I0829773
CHILDREN LEARNING BOOKS
Alligator
Jessica Cheong

ISBN: 9781795003629

Hi, my name is Charlie. I am an alligator. Want to learn more about me and my friends?

We are
reptiles and
we are cold-
blooded. We
gain body heat
by sunbathing.

We are
divided into
two species,
the American
alligator, and
the Chinese
alligator.

We live in freshwater environments, such as ponds, marshes, wetlands, rivers, and swamps.

We eat a wide range of animals that we can find near our habitats, such as fish, birds, turtles and sometimes deer.

Male alligators are larger than female alligators. The average size for a female alligator is 8.2 feet (2.6 meters), and the average size for a male alligator is 11.2 feet (3.4 meters).

1000 lb

We can
weigh
over
1000 lb
(454 kg).

65 Days

Alligator eggs hatch after 65 days of incubation.

Cold
Hot

Our eggs become male or female depending on the temperature, male in warmer temperature and female in cooler temperatures.

6-8" (15-20cm)

Baby alligators are about 6 to 8 inches (15 to 20 centimeters) when they hatch.

We are very smart. We don't make the same mistake twice.

We have between 74 and 80 teeth in our mouth at a time. As our teeth wear down, they are replaced. We can go through 3000 teeth in a lifetime.

We can live up approximately 50 years.

Thank You

I hope you enjoy reading this book. Please leave an honest review on Amazon.

My Books

All my books are available in Amazon Kindle and Paperback. They are all enrolled in Kindle Unlimited and Kindle Owners' Lending Library.

You can visit my author page:

http://www.amazon.com/author/jessicacheong

Children Story Books:

1. **Children Story Books – Ella's Day at Kindergarten**
   Kindle ASIN: B075VTPNVV
   Paperback ASIN: 1549813471
   Paperback ISBN: 9781549813474

2. **Children Story Books – Ella At The Beach**
   Kindle ASIN: B077QJL5VF
   Paperback ASIN: 1973376520
   Paperback ISBN: 9781973376521

Children Learning Books:

1. **Animals in Alphabets and Their Habitats**
   Kindle ASIN: B06XDLML3L
   Paperback ASIN: 1520746725
   Paperback ISBN: 9781520746722

2. **Children Learning Books – Ant**
   Kindle ASIN: B079Q8V57J
   Paperback ASIN: 1980247935
   Paperback ISBN: 9781980247937

3. **Children Learning Books – Alligator**
   Kindle ASIN: B07N2B4YNY
   Paperback ASIN: 1795003626
   Paperback ISBN: 9781795003629